MW00438320

Visions
&
Dreams

Recognizing God's Supernatural Signs

GARY OATES
with
Robert Paul Lamb

Open Heaven Publications
an outreach of Gary Oates Ministries, Inc.
P.O. Box 457/Moravian Falls, NC 28654
336-667-2333

Visions & Dreams

Copyright © 2014 by Gary Oates Ministries, Inc.

ISBN 978-0-9752622-2-X

Requests for information should be directed to:

Open Heaven Publications
an outreach of Gary Oates Ministries, Inc.
P.O. Box 457/Moravian Falls, NC 28654
336-667-2333

Printed in the United States of America

*"...Write the vision and engrave it so plainly
upon tablets that everyone who passes
may [be able to] read [it easily and quickly]
as he hastens by."*

Habakkuk 2:2
Amplified Bible

Table of Contents

Introduction

Does God give visions to people today?

I say emphatically "yes". Not only is that true of believers but to unbelievers as well.

Many of us have heard of incredibly dramatic stories of unbelievers and those of other religions living in remote areas of the world who have given their lives to Jesus directly as a result of experiencing a supernatural vision or dream.

The problem is that the established church in various places in America or Europe has become a "spectator sport". Some want a leader—either a prophet or a pastor—to seek God on their behalf. A comfortable few want to be "spoon-fed" the Gospel.

The simple truth is that we must all work hand-in-hand with the Holy Spirit to develop our spiritual senses. It is critical that we have *experiential* knowledge about the things of the Spirit, as well as head knowledge of the Bible.

Unquestionably, most believers have had more supernatural encounters with God than they think they have. As well, many Christians have also had more visions and, for the most part, they didn't realize those manifestations were from God.

That's why all believers desperately need the discerning of spirits working in their lives (1 Corinthians 12:10). That spiritual gift is one of the nine manifestations of the Holy Spirit which clearly helps us to know what is from God and what is not.

More specifically, the discerning of spirits is the supernatural ability to discern the spirit world and its activities, and especially to have spiritual insight into the true motives of people.

Vision is the root word for visualization, but please understand that visualization is not based in some fuzzy New Age theory. It basically means using one's sanctified imagination, and visualizing images on the screen of your mind.

I have come to believe that spiritual sight is a higher level of seeing than natural physical sight. Listen to the admonition of 2 Corinthians 4:18:

"While we look not at the things which are seen, but at the things which are not seen; for the things which are seen are temporal, but the things which are not seen are eternal."

That instruction commends looking beyond the natural physical world into the realm of the Spirit, the areas not visible to the naked eye. The things we can see with our physical eyes are temporary. They will crumble and be gone one day.

But the Spirit realm exists forever.

Hebrews 11:27 says of the mighty prophet Moses, *"...he endured as seeing Him who is unseen."* In essence, he was not looking at his circumstances as he led God's people out of Egyptian slavery into the land of promise. He was looking into the eternal realm.

I have personally discovered the spirit world is more real and more powerful than the natural physical world that we live in. After all, the visible world was created out of the invisible realm.

That truth is well established in Hebrews 11:3 (NKJV), *"By faith we understand that the worlds were framed by the word of God, so that the things which are seen were not made of things which are visible."*

The ancient Book of Job, often considered the oldest book in the entire Bible, acknowledges this magnificent gift of spiritual sight in Job 42:5 (Amplified). *"I had heard of You [only] by the hearing of the ear, but now my [spiritual] eye sees You."*

The Spirit Filled Life Bible adds an insightful comment on that passage. "Job...compares his former knowledge of God, which had come from others—the hearing of the ear—with his present knowledge, which is superior because it has come directly—now my eye sees. He sees God differently because of personal revelation."

Clearly, the ability to see with spiritual eyes is more superior than with natural sight. However, that gifting to be able to "see" into the realm of the Spirit only comes through personal revelation of the Spirit of God Himself.

As new born believers in Jesus, most of us have been satisfied with simply being able to see with our natural sight. But there is a greater realm available for us as children of God.

There is another, greater dimension. It is a place where God develops our spiritual sight—our sanctified imagination—and enables us to receive heavenly visions causing us to flow in supernatural manifestations from our Creator.

Come and join me in this Spirit-led journey.

Gary Oates
Moravian Falls, NC

Chapter 1

Visions in the Night

"Hold fast to the vision God gives you early in life. Do not divert from it. God can bring it to pass."

--Spirit Filled Life Bible
Truth-In-Action (Genesis)

My dreams haunted me for years.

The flickering and troubling images in my nightly dreams disturbed me for most of my childhood. At times, I dreaded the very thought of going to sleep at night because of the upsetting dreams which were seemingly ever-present.

Perhaps these visions of the night would have frightened anyone as I seemingly stood before a vast sea of faces—people appearing from all races—and preached the Gospel. It appeared to be thousands of people. Night after night the dreams came.

Visions & Dreams

But the great mystery was that I was eight years old, and not yet a Christian. What did these dreams mean? How could all of those images be real? Why would I be dreaming of such things?

I wasn't qualified to do things like that. My mental excuses were endless. I was just an introverted boy, and certainly too shy and insecure to stand before people of any kind and do much talking.

Of course, I attended church. My God-fearing, Baptist parents saw to that. I had even spoken once in church on a "youth Sunday", but I was not a believer in the typical evangelical sense.

I had never walked an aisle and professed faith in Jesus. I was fearful of ever taking *that* step—for surely, if I did, that meant I would have to preach exactly as I'd seen myself doing in those nightly visions.

Honestly, I feared that giving my life to Jesus would set the stage for me going to Africa as a missionary. It was *that* clear in my mind.

The never-ending, frustrating struggle continued for years until at fourteen, I finally—reluctantly— surrendered to the Lord. It all began with hearing a visiting pastor explain what it truly meant to become a believer. That night at home, I made the biggest commitment of my life.

I made a total surrender of my life to God. "I'll even go to Africa and preach if that's what You want," I promised the Lord.

Visions in the Night

Even though time seemingly passed in the blink of an eye, the dreams of preaching to those faceless crowds always remained in the back of my mind.

Or, you could say it was a quantum leap forward into the fast-paced 21st Century from the "laid-back" days of being reared in a small Florida town in the early 1950s.

It was now 2002, and some fifty years had passed since those nightly dreams of my Florida childhood. After a recent dramatic encounter with the Holy Spirit, I had traveled with a ministry team led by revivalist Randy Clark to the sprawling city of Belem on the northeast coast of Brazil, a mere hundred miles from the Atlanta Ocean.

In a hotel ballroom in downtown Belem, Randy and I began laying hands on our team members in preparation for a giant rally that night at a large soccer stadium. It was always a time of impartation before the actual services took place. We then came back together and laid hands on each other in prayer.

All of a sudden ...baaaammmmm!

It was like a bolt of electricity hit us at the very same moment and we both tumbled onto the floor. I never even remembered hitting the floor but I was gone immediately from the power of God touching my physical body.

Instantly, I saw an angel walking up to me. He

was a brilliant golden color and had the face of a man. The look on his face was one of seriousness but it also held the wondrous attributes of compassion and gentleness. He was carrying a scepter in his hand which he gave me, and then he took a crown from his head and placed it upon mine.

As quickly as he appeared, the angel turned and walked away.

Time passed slowly. I was a slobbering wreck on the floor. Seeing my condition, Randy had to get the ministry team to the stadium. "Everybody get on the bus," he instructed. "Gary and the others can take a taxi."

Shaken and trembling from what had happened, I found myself awash from tears, sweat and snot. I lay in a crumpled state on the floor for a long time. When I finally was able to stand, I realized the ballroom was empty.

Everyone seemed to have left me.

Then, I heard some muffled noise behind several large columns in the ballroom and discovered my wife Kathi and two other people—all struggling to stand on their feet as well. It wasn't just me getting left. There were three more including my wife!

One of the girls could speak Portuguese so she got us a taxi and we were hurriedly driven to the stadium. Worship had already begun by the time we had arrived. The four of us were still exceedingly dizzy from our experiences at the ballroom.

Visions in the Night

A large wooden platform had been built in the middle of the stadium and I had to intentionally concentrate on every step to keep my footing as I walked onto the stage.

Randy met me on the platform saying, "We're going to tag team tonight...I'm going to start and you finish."

"Sure," I mumbled, unsure of what I could actually do in that state of spiritual stupor. It seemed as if I was totally unprepared. I hadn't even brought my Bible with me to the stadium. But God instantly gave me understanding and anointing for what He wanted done.

The next thing I knew I was up preaching with the Brazilian interpreter. A boldness and confidence in God I had never experienced before saturated my entire being.

"God is calling you to friendship with him tonight. He loves you. That's why he died on the cross that you might receive forgiveness of sins... that you might experience new life. You can be free from the shackles and the bondages of sin in your life. The chains of bondage can be broken tonight. You can be set free. You can be free to serve God with your whole heart."

The people roared with shouts of approval.

"I am calling you to demonstrate your love for God," I continued. "I am calling you to repentance. I am calling you to come now. Get up from where you are and run down here quickly."

It seemed the noise of the crowd was even louder.

"By coming here, you are saying I am no longer a friend of the world," I preached. "I am making myself a friend of God. I am no longer a friend of the world."

Over 5,000 people responded that night to the altar call, and at least one thousand of them made a first time commitment to Jesus.

I had never preached under that kind of potent and compelling Holy Spirit-directed unction in my whole life. In fact, I had never done anything like that before—*ever*!

As a pastor for many years, I had always led small, fledgling congregations of a hundred or less. Mostly less! Now, I was standing before thousands in a foreign nation and preaching the Gospel with power and authority.

In truth I had received a supernatural impartation from the golden angel to give that heavenly message on "Friendship with God".

That incredible service in Brazil was the fulfillment of the vision I had been given fifty years earlier. In fact, several years would pass before I ever connected the two experiences.

Even later, I realized that Belem is the Portuguese word for "Bethlehem", the little town of Jesus' birth.

I too had experienced an incredible birthing in the "fruitful house of bread"—Bethlehem.

But God is always faithful and true to bring to pass whatever He has promised!

Chapter 2

What Is A Vision?

"...We look not at the things which are seen, but at the things which are not seen; for the things which are seen are temporal, but the things which are not seen are eternal."

-- 2 Corinthians 4:18 (NASB)

What is a vision?

A vision is simply a mental image or a picture that is projected on the screen of a person's mind. That sounds a lot like imagination, doesn't it? What is imagination? It's the forming of mental images.

During a recent time of study, I looked up the word *"vision"* in the Merriam-Webster Dictionary. The first definition caught me by surprise because it's an important spiritual definition of vision. That definition is: "something seen in a dream, trance or ecstasy, especially a supernatural experience that conveys a revelation."

The second definition of *"vision"* from Merriam-Webster is: "a thought, concept or object formed by the imagination. The act or power of imagination."

Job 33:14-16 importantly calls our attention to the basic difference between a vision and a dream.

"Indeed God speaks once, or twice, yet no one notices it. In a dream <u>a vision of the night</u>, when sound sleep falls on men, while they slumber in their beds, then He opens the ears of men, and seals their instructions."

A dream is a form of a vision but it occurs while a person is sleeping. We have visions in the day time and dreams at night. Yet, it is exactly the same mechanism utilizing the screen of one's mind where these images appear.

Note the expression *"yet no one notices it."* God is speaking to His people; yet, they are failing to hear.

Most Christians would argue they haven't heard God's voice—perhaps ever. But that statement runs contrary to the words of Jesus when He said *"My sheep hear My voice,"* (John 10:27).

As believers, we all have the capability of hearing God's voice. The problem is that many of the Lord's people have not *discerned* His voice. They have not acknowledged that He was speaking in their inner-most being. The great tendency is to simply override the voice of God with one's own thoughts.

What Is A Vision?

But this fundamental point is well established: if you are a believer in Jesus, you can hear the voice of God.

A Prophet's Hearing

As a close friend of the late Bob Jones, who was recognized as a valid prophet throughout the world-wide Body of Christ, I know personally that he received constant revelation from God by way of both visions and dreams.

How does that happen in a person's life?

I believe the Spirit of the Lord teaches and trains that person over an extended period of time to hear and respond to His voice. The time frame of that training usually covers many years.

Numbers 12:6 (NASB) establishes God's principle and also the means of delivering a revelatory word through a prophetic messenger. *"If there is a prophet among you, I, the Lord, shall make Myself known to him in a vision. I shall speak with him in a dream."*

That kind of training is basic to those with apostolic or prophetic callings. But this experience is available for every one of us as Christians (according to Joel 2:28 and Acts 2:17).

The prophet Joel first prophesied these events occurring at a critical point in time, and Peter wisely acknowledged them when they happened on the Day of Pentecost.

Visions & Dreams

"And it shall come to pass in the last days, says God, that I will pour out of My Spirit on all flesh; Your sons and your daughters shall prophesy, Your young men shall see visions, Your old men shall dream dreams," (NKJV).

The Value of Visions

For a long time, I completely misunderstood the truth of Proverbs 29:18. It says *"where there is no vision, the people perish"* (KJV).

I always thought that verse meant that we should have a purpose and a goal for our lives. As a former pastor, who had the privilege of planting five different churches in states from Washington to Florida, I was goal-oriented and accustomed to making detailed plans for the churches I led. We called them "five year plans".

But that is not what this particular verse is addressing. The New American Standard Bible states: *"Where there is no vision, the people are unrestrained."*

The New King James Version says: *"Where there is no revelation, the people cast off restraint."*

The Hebrew word, which is translated *revelation*, literally means "prophetic vision".

The Amplified Bible captures a more accurate understanding of that simple expression *"no vision"* to actually mean *"no redemptive revelation of God."*

What Is A Vision?

Thus, we can reasonably conclude Proverbs 29:18 is talking about spiritual visions—not goals and purposes for living.

I am absolutely convinced that we must see visions on a regular basis to keep us on the cutting edge of what God is doing in the earthly realm. Without that kind of clear vision, we become unrestrained, have little purpose and can fail in our calling.

The Message Bible presents Proverbs 29:18 in this manner: *"If people can't see what God is doing, they stumble all over themselves; but when they attend to what He reveals, they are most blessed."*

Jesus established the right pattern of conduct between the Father and Himself in John 5:19. *"I only do what I see My Father do,"* He said. As children of God, we have the ability to see what our Father is doing in the realm of the Spirit, and to cooperate with Him in touching countless lives wherever we go upon this earth.

Visions & God's Timing

The prophet Habakkuk makes this insightful prediction. *"For the vision is yet for the appointed time; it hastens toward the goal and it will not fail. Though it tarries, wait for it; for it will certainly come, it will not delay',"* (Habakkuk 2:3).

These words from Habakkuk almost sound like spiritual double talk. The vision *"hastens"* but *"wait for it."* Somehow *"it tarries"* but *"will not delay."*

Visions & Dreams

Many of the prophets in the Bible never lived to see any of the fulfillments of their visions. It can also be accurately stated that some of those visions have yet to come to pass after thousands of years.

Undoubtedly, the Holy Spirit is the best interpreter of visions and dreams. Truly, God can bring revelation to you about these supernatural experiences that you have had.

As we diligently seek Him, I believe revelation and understanding will be released. That may happen immediately or gradually depending upon God's timing for your life but—trust me—it will happen.

Peter's Vision

The book of Acts gives us the unusual story of the apostle Peter going up on a housetop about noon one day to pray, and a supernatural event unfolded that would forever change church history.

"And he became hungry, and was desiring to eat, but while they were making preparations, <u>he fell into a trance</u>;

'and he saw the sky opened up, and an object like a great sheet coming down, lowered by four corners to the ground,

"and there were in it all kinds of four-footed animals and crawling creatures of the earth and birds of the air.

"A voice came to him, 'Get up, Peter, kill and eat'!"

24

What Is A Vision?

(Acts 10:10-13).

As an observant Jew, he was appalled at such a command. *"By no means, Lord for I have never eaten anything unholy and unclean,"* (Acts 10:14). This scene in Peter's vision was repeated three times before it was taken up, and the Bible records that he was *"greatly perplexed"* over what had happened and spent three days seeking God for answers.

Those answers for Peter connected him to the centurion Cornelius who had just experienced an angelic visitation himself. When Peter took a step of faith and followed the summons to the house of Cornelius, he stepped into a setting where the church world as he had known it was about to be turned upside down.

"I most certainly understand now that God is not one to show partiality," Peter declared (Acts 10:34), now standing in the light of his vision.

The apostle Peter was the first disciple to preach the Gospel to a house filled with Gentiles, who promptly received a great outpouring of the Holy Spirit (Acts 10:44). His supernatural experience in the vision was God's *confirmed* guidance that the Gospel of Jesus Christ was now open to the Gentiles of the earth.

Peter's ministry among the Gentiles violated every religious tradition he had ever known as a Jew. But that all changed when he understood God's vision.

Chapter 3

Visions in the Scriptures

"If there is a prophet among you, I, the Lord, shall make Myself known to him in a vision. I shall speak with him in a dream."

--Numbers 12:6 (NASB)

A thorough study of the Scripture often brings us to the uncanny realization we have misread various passages, and arrived at conclusions that cannot be supported by a closer examination.

That is especially true if a person was raised in a particular denomination which did not recognize the gifts of the Holy Spirit being valid for today. In such cases those passages were simply written off.

For instance, I have discovered some passages that occurred *"in a vision"* and not the way I first thought they had happened. I found that visions in the Bible were much more common than I realized.

Let's consider the following stories from both the Old Testament and New Testament as we examine powerful visions in the lives of God's people.

Abram's Vision

Genesis 15 details the remarkable story of God's unprecedented visit with Abram. This encounter with the Almighty occurs before Abram's name is changed to Abraham.

"And He took him outside and said 'Now look toward the heavens and count the stars, if you are able to count them.' And He said to him, 'So shall your descendants be','" (verse 5).

My original concept of that passage was that God Himself came to Abram, *physically* took him outside and pointed up to the sky and said "look at the stars..."

You might have thought the same thing.

But that's not what the Bible actually says, according to Genesis 15:1. *"After these things the word of the Lord came to Abram in a vision, saying 'Do not fear, Abram, I am a shield to you; your reward shall be very great'."*

Here is Abram's story in a nutshell. He had a vision in which God Himself appeared to him and promised something in the natural dimension that was completely impossible. Yet, Abram believed what God had said in the vision and that it was from the living God.

Abram's faith in what God promised became an absolute reality, and the Bible declares, *"and he believed in the Lord and He reckoned it to him as righteousness"* (Genesis 15:6).

Contrary to being childless, advanced in age and having no heir in the natural, Abram was given a total fulfillment of that God-given promise. That divine provision became an achieved destiny against all odds, and he became *"the father of all who believe"* (Romans 4:17).

Samuel's Vision

Another magnificent story of receiving direction from God in a vision comes from 1 Samuel 3:1-15 where we are told *"The word of the Lord was rare...in those days; there was no frequent or widely spread vision,"* (verse 1, Amplified Bible).

As Samuel lay down upon his bed to sleep, the Lord called him by name. Immediately, the young boy thought it was Eli calling to him. Yet, the elderly priest said he had not called the lad.

This scenario was repeated three times before Eli finally said *"Go lie down, and it shall be if He calls you, that you shall say, 'Speak, Lord for Thy servant is listening',"* (verse 9).

The Hebrew word here for *listening* in verses 9 and 10 literally means "to listen with the intent to obey." This is *serious* listening. It's a special level of listening that we offer to God alone.

And, the proper response is: "Whatever You say, I am going to obey. I'm going to obey Your Word."

I always looked at this story of Samuel's first intimate encounter with the Lord as if He was standing right there beside the young boy's bed. At least that's the impression I drew from reading verse 10 which gives the impression that the entire event happened in the natural.

Yet, a proper reading of verse 15 conveys an often overlooked detail here. *"But Samuel was afraid to tell the vision to Eli."*

God's appearance to the young boy, Samuel was clearly in a vision.

The Vision on the Mount

Matthew 17:1-9 is another passage of Scripture that has often been misread or misunderstood. In this case, Peter, James and John went up on the Mount of Transfiguration with Jesus, *"and His face shone like the sun, and His garments became as white as light,"* (verse 2).

Then, Moses and Elijah unexpectedly appeared and began talking with Jesus. Theologians agree that the appearance of Moses and Elijah demonstrates that the Law and the Prophets support Jesus in His redemptive mission for mankind.

But as Jesus and the three disciples come down from the mountain, He commanded them: *"Tell the vision to no one until the Son of Man is risen from the dead,"* (verse 9).

Bible scholars have debated this passage for a considerable time. Some suggesting that the Greek word *orama* ("vision") is simply that which is seen.

However, a majority of theological books including the highly-regarded Strong's Concordance presents *orama* in supernatural terms saying it is "a sight divinely granted in an ecstasy or in sleep." From Strong's point of view, it is "a vision."

And, for my part, I agree with Strong's!

Zacharias in the Temple

Luke 1:9-23 gives us the account of the angel Gabriel appearing to the priest Zacharias who *"was performing his priestly service before God in the appointed order of his division,"* (verse 9).

Notice that Gabriel was at the temple for a special mission at a specific moment in time. *"Do not be afraid, Zacharias, for your petition has been heard, and your wife Elizabeth will bear you a son, and you will give him the name John,"* (verse 10).

Even though he was a righteous man married to Elizabeth, a woman in the lineage of Aaron, Zacharias was clearly overwhelmed with the angel's news. He was an old man and his wife *"advanced in years,"* according to verse 18.

Visions & Dreams

Because he looked at his natural circumstances and did not believe Gabriel's words, the angel said *"you shall be silent and unable to speak until the day when these things take place...,"* (verse 20).

And, when Zacharias finally stepped from the temple, he was unable to speak to the people awaiting him. It was then that the people suddenly *"realized that he had seen a vision in the temple; and he kept making signs to them, and remained mute,"* (verse 22).

Zacharias was unable to speak until the day that his son, John the Baptist was born. His mouth was opened, his tongue loosed, and he began to speak God's praise.

He was also filled with the Holy Spirit and prophesied that John would *"be called the prophet of the Most High"* and would *"go on before the Lord to prepare His ways,"* (verse 76).

Yet, the heart of Zacharias' angelic encounter all came about in a vision.

Women at the Tomb

Luke 24 tells us the brief story of two men walking seven miles from Jerusalem to Emmaus when the resurrected *"Jesus Himself drew near and went with them,"* (verse 15, NKJV).

Because their eyes were "restrained", they began to explain to the Lord how Jesus of Nazareth "was a prophet mighty in deed and word before God" and was crucified.

Three days have now passed, according to the men. *"...and certain women of our company, who arrived at the tomb early, astonished us. When they did not find His body, they came saying that they had also seen <u>a vision</u> of angels who said He was alive,"* (verses 22-23).

The angelic vision to the women that Jesus was alive proved true to the two men walking with Jesus when *"their eyes were opened and they knew Him...,"* (verse 31).

What the women saw was in a vision!

Paul's Vision

Acts 16 unfolds the details of Paul, Silas and Timothy's missionary trip to Phrygia and Galatia when the Lord began to give precise instructions about their journey, *"having been forbidden by the Holy Spirit to speak the word in Asia"* (verse 6, NASB).

In Mysia and while attempting to go into Bithynia, they got the same message: *"the Spirit of Jesus did not permit them"* (verse 7)

They persevered in seeking the Lord's direction and finally their plans were made clear when they finally reached Troas.

"A <u>vision</u> appeared to Paul in the night; a man of Macedonia was standing and appealing to him, and

saying, 'Come over to Macedonia and help us.
"And when he had seen the vision, immediately
we sought to go into Macedonia, concluding that God
had called us to preach the gospel to them," (verses
9-10).

This is an impressive story to me in several ways.
First, Paul and his team didn't attempt to ignore the
specific direction the Holy Spirit was giving to them.

Secondly, it doesn't say that an angel appeared
and gave directions for Paul's team to go into
Macedonia. No, it was a common, ordinary man
who made the appeal <u>in a vision</u>, and they wisely
decided to head for Macedonia.

Please understand this important truth. We
can't confine our supernatural guidance to simply
angelic messengers showing up with the precise
details at the *right* time as we need them.

Some of us might have potentially missed God's
direction in this case because of the common
quality of Paul's guidance. But it proved incredibly
accurate and true!

Paul at Corinth

The apostle Paul faced unbelievable challenges
in his itinerant ministry of preaching the Gospel.

In 2 Corinthians 11:23-26 (NKJV), he details
some of those experiences:

"...in stripes above measure, in prisons more

frequently, in deaths often.
"From the Jews five times I received forty stripes minus one.

"Three times I was beaten with rods; once I was stoned; three times I was shipwrecked; a night and a day I have been in the deep;

"in journeys often, in perils of waters, in perils of robbers, in perils of my own countrymen..."

Obviously, a man of God such as Paul would have to carefully follow the guidance of the Holy Spirit in where he went and how he conducted himself.

In Acts 17, we are told of Paul's ministry efforts in Thessalonica, Berea and Athens—even preaching upon Mars Hill. After some minimal success there, Paul left Athens and went to Corinth (Acts 18:1). It was in Corinth that he began to reason in the synagogue every Sabbath *"testifying to the Jews that Jesus was the Christ"* (verses 4-5).

A revival broke out as he, Silas and Timothy ministered. *"Crispus, the leader of the synagogue, believed in the Lord with all his household, and many of the Corinthians when they heard were believing and being baptized,"* (Acts 18:8).

Obviously, the Lord desired Paul to settle down in Corinth for a season and plant a new church. So, He sent divine instructions. Listen to the words of Acts 18:9-10 regarding those directions.

"And the Lord said to Paul in the night <u>by a vision</u>, 'Do not be afraid any longer, but go on speaking and do not be silent;

"for I am with you, and no man will attack you

in order to harm you, for I have many people in this city."

It would prove one of Paul's most successful times of ministry as he stayed in Corinth over a year and six months, teaching the word of God among them. But the direction for that ministry period came from heaven "by a vision".

Paul at Jerusalem

Upon his arrest at the temple in Jerusalem, Paul actually gets permission from the Roman commander to speak to the mob wanting to kill him (Acts 21:40). He then began telling the story of his dramatic encounter with Jesus on the road to Damascus and his healing from blindness.

Years before Paul returned to Jerusalem from that life-changing experience and gave this account:

"It happened when I returned to Jerusalem and was praying in the temple, that I fell into a trance,
"and I saw Him saying to me, 'Make haste, and get out of Jerusalem quickly, because they will not accept your testimony about Me'," (Acts 22:17-18).

His ministry always involved God's supernatural.

Chapter 4

A Vision in the Morning

"In the third year of Cyrus king of Persia a message was revealed to Daniel, who was named Belteshazzar; and the message was true and one of great conflict, but he understood the message and had an understanding of the vision."

-- Daniel 10:1 (NASB)

The first Monday morning of June 1975 I had what I considered a rare and unusual vision. At the time, my wife Kathi and I were living in Leavenworth, Washington where we were planting our first church when I had a vision of hovering (as in a helicopter) over the city of Gatlinburg, Tennessee.

I saw the downtown area of Gatlinburg, the space needle and surrounding mountain terrain of the Great Smokies. In the midst of that vision, I heard the voice of God speaking to me: "Go to Gatlinburg and begin a ministry."

Immediately, I thought, "No. That's not God talking to me. There's no way I could do that."

When Kathi awoke, I told her about the vision. "No, that's not God," she said emphatically.

We had only been in Leavenworth for three years and absolutely loved the area. Why would we want to leave? The church was growing and all was well with the world. The nearby Cascade Mountains were beautiful and we had no desire to move anywhere else.

But I was troubled about the voice of God and the vision of what I saw was so vivid and strong. There was real clarity to every part of what the Lord said to me. Finally, I told the Lord in prayer, "If this is You...You are *really* going to have to confirm this direction for us."

We determined that we would not say a word to anybody about my experience—and we didn't. Absolutely nobody knew anything about our plans.

But a couple of days later we were shopping in a small grocery store. When I got to the checkout counter, the cashier was a woman I had never seen before. As she finished ringing up our groceries, she looked at me and said, "I heard you all are moving to Gatlinburg, Tennessee."

"What did you say?" I mumbled in disbelief.

"Yeah, I heard you're moving to Gatlinburg, Tennessee," she repeated.

A Vision in the Morning

I was completely stunned, almost speechless. Neither Kathi nor I had told a soul about my experience. We were both still in the valley of decision.

Of course, we talked a long time later about the mysterious cashier. Who was *that* woman?

There were several other confirmations including a dairyman from whom we bought raw milk. It seems he grew up in the Gatlinburg area and was often talking about his "home" back there.

I was somewhat familiar with the Gatlinburg area in eastern Tennessee having traveled there from Florida several times with my family to attend a nearby youth camp.

Finally, I decided to write the Chamber of Commerce in Gatlinburg and inquire about churches in the area. Were there any Charismatic congregations there? I ultimately got a letter back saying they didn't know what kind of church I was talking about, but they did have some "nice" denominational churches.

One day while my letter was still sitting on the desk of the Chamber's manager, a woman came into the office to retrieve some flyers. "You may want to see this man's letter," the manager suggested. The woman read my letter inquiring about churches and she decided to write me.

"I have a small home group meeting in my house and we have been praying that God would send us a pastor," she wrote. "Why don't you pray about coming here?"

Her letter was the clincher.

Three months later we sold everything we owned and moved across the country to Gatlinburg without knowing a single person there except Maria Bruni, the woman who'd written us.

We began holding meetings with her group teaching about the gifts of the Spirit and the baptism with the Holy Spirit. Lives were promptly changed and souls came into God's kingdom. We began baptizing people in the river who had given their lives to Jesus.

Shortly thereafter, a visibly upset Maria came to me one day. "I didn't know anything about your doctrine when you came here," she said. "I don't believe any of this stuff you're preaching. That's not where we're going."

I suppose I should have known a problem would come. Maria managed an evangelical bookstore that did not allow charismatic books. The Lord had already told me that I shouldn't build on another man's foundation, and I told Maria that.

She was still unhappy about everything.

"God used you to get us here and He evidently has a purpose in all of that," I explained. "We want to do everything with the highest integrity so we'll move across town and restart our meetings there.

A Vision in the Morning

We will not compete with your group in any way."

That seemed agreeable with her.

In the meanwhile, the hand of God was being seen mightily in Gatlinburg. Drug addicts, drug dealers, prostitutes and even witch doctors were giving their hearts to Jesus.

We began an event called "Gatlinburg Gathering" on the 4th of July renting the local civic center for services with well-known Christian personalities. In time, the "700 Club" came to town and did a segment on our church and the lives of people who had been so dramatically touched by the Lord.

About two years later, Maria—the woman who had first invited us to Gatlinburg—came to me in tears. "Forgive me," she said. "I see the fruit of your ministry. It's obvious God is greatly blessing what you're doing here."

"I want everything God has for me," she declared.

That very day, Maria received the infilling of the Holy Spirit, and at the same time, God awakened and released great spiritual gifts in her life. The church God led us across the country to plant in Gatlinburg became her spiritual foundation.

In time, she decided to return to her native country of Austria where she married businessman Herbert Prean and launched a ministry that began almost immediately to flourish throughout the continent. She ministered effectively in Germany,

Switzerland and Austria and throughout Europe.

After Herbert's passing, her travels increased and her ministry continued to expand. For years, she was a keynote speaker at "The Feast of Tabernacles" in Jerusalem. In some places her notoriety became equivalent to that of someone like Joyce Meyer notoriety in the USA.

In 2001, she went to Kampala, Uganda and built a training center, a school, a hospital and a huge orphanage. She told me recently that her property in Uganda that God had blessed them with contains over 100 buildings. Her ministry there is called "Vision for Africa" and has wonderfully touched thousands of lives.

A few years ago I was in Imst, Austria ministering with her, and she graciously introduced me as "her *first* pastor". In the eyes of her people, I was an instant hero as her pastor.

But I had never looked at the remarkable situation with Maria quite like that.

For me, God gave an unusual vision and some basic directions to follow. We got out of the boat and followed Him to Tennessee from Washington State. In the process, Maria got touched in such an incredible way that God has used her as a "nation changer" in diverse places from Austria to Uganda.

But it all started with a simple vision one morning in Washington State...and thousands of people got touched all along the way.

And for all that God accomplished, I can honestly shout: "Praise the Lord!"

Chapter 5

False Visions & Prophets

"Beware of the false prophets, who come to you in sheep's clothing, but inwardly are ravenous wolves. You will know them by their fruits..."

-- Matthew 7:15-16 (NASB)

Did you know a *true* prophet of God can be wrong?

It may surprise some believers but being incorrect does not make that person a false prophet. However, it does make them a *wrong* prophet.

The late Bob Jones was a good example of that statement. In many ways, he was the most unconventional minister of the Gospel I have ever known. An uneducated man who dropped out in grammar school, he was nonetheless a brilliant man. He traveled widely and impacted thousands of lives throughout the world. His encouragement to people was legendary.

Even more important, he probably had the best track record of anybody I've worked with in ministry for prophetic accuracy. He was just simply un-believable in that arena.

But when he ever missed a prophetic word, he was humble enough to admit it. That was certainly the case in 2012 when he announced that he believed Mitt Romney was God's choice in that year's presidential election.

"I thought it was God," I've heard him admit, "but I misinterpreted what God was saying."

That didn't make him a false prophet. It made him an *incorrect* prophet on that point.

Just as there are true visions from God, there are also false visions from the enemy to lead us down a path of deception. Please consider the words of Jeremiah 14:14 (NASB) in that regard.

"The prophets are prophesying falsehood in My name. I have neither sent them nor commanded them nor spoken to them; they are prophesying to you a false vision, divination, futility and the deception of their own minds."

What is "the deception of their own minds?"

It's essentially believing a lie and acting as though it's actually true. Truthfully, you can hear whatever you want to hear and happily tell others,

"God told me." Yet, God might have only spoken a brief word to you, or nothing at all.

Such was the case of a false prophet by the name of Balaam, who not only blessed Israel and prophesied the coming of the Messiah (Numbers 10-11, 17-19), but caused the death of 24,000 because they followed his counsel (Numbers 25:1-9).

Two apostles—Peter and Jude—both address the sins of Balaam (2 Peter 2:15-16, Jude 11). But so does Revelation 2:14, addressing those in the church at Pergamum, *"who hold the teaching of Balaam, who kept teaching Balak to put a stumbling block before the sons of Israel, to eat things sacrificed to idols and to commit acts of immorality."*

False teachers and false prophets were prevalent in the Scriptures. And they are with us today.

In this day when there is such an incredible outpouring of the Holy Spirit throughout the whole earth, we must be able to rightly discern what we are seeing and hearing so that we might *not* be led astray.

This is where the "discerning of spirits" is critically needed. I believe it is the most necessary gift of the nine gifts of the Holy Spirit (1 Cor. 12:7-11) for the church today. Without that gifting, believers are open to all kinds of false doctrines, false visions and unbiblical religious practices, and are easily manipulated and misled by the cunning and craftiness of errant teachers.

47

Visions & Dreams

There is so much "spiritual junk" happening among God's people in this hour. It absolutely requires acute discerning of spirits to know what is from God and what is from the devil.

I have known situations where people have spoken astounding prophetic words, and then these very same people attempted to make their own predicttions happen. Often times, they will manipulate and attempt to influence events to make it appear their words are accurate.

Yet, the failure of such questionable prophesying is a foregone conclusion here.

The prophet Daniel predicts of a time when there will be violent people who *"will also lift themselves up in order to fulfill the vision, but they will fall down,"* (Daniel 11:14).

I am convinced—after many years of ministry— every true vision from God will inevitably come to pass. It might occur in my lifetime or yours, but it will happen.

For instance, Bob Jones prophesied about that devastating underground earthquake and tsunami in Japan that happened in 2011. Bob's word, however, came twenty years *before* it occurred.

People dismissed Bob and his prophecy because the earthquake didn't occur right after it was predicted. He was kicked out of churches and even some ministerial groups sent him packing. People seemingly didn't want him around anymore because he was viewed as a false prophet.

Then, the earthquake and the resulting tsunami struck Japan creating devastation and killing thousands of lives exactly as Bob had said. The *detailed* accuracy of his prophecy was astonishing. A number of people immediately came back to Bob with apologies. "We were the ones in the wrong," many of them admitted.

God's time frame for events and our time frame can be totally different in seeing a prophetic word fulfilled. Yet, if the prophecy or vision is legitimate, God has a precise timing involved.

Ezekiel 12:23 (NASB) confirms that significant truth. *"The days draw near as well as the fulfillment of every vision."*

Revelation 22:20 (NASB) is the next to the last verse in the Bible and contains a sovereign promise from the Lord Jesus. *"Yes, I am coming quickly."*

That statement was made over 2,000 years ago, which doesn't sound like a very prompt return to me. However, 2 Peter 3:8 (NASB) tells us *"...with the Lord one day is as a thousand years, and a thousand years as one day."*

In that sense of divine timing, the Lord Jesus made that statement only two days ago!

Understanding Visions & Dreams

The prophet Habakkuk makes this insightful

prediction about God's timing with fulfilled visions. *"For the vision is yet for the appointed time; it hastens toward the goal and it will not fail. Though it tarries, wait for it; for it will certainly come, it will not delay,"* (Habakkuk 2:3, NASB).

There are many books presently available on the subject of interpreting visions and dreams, and some of them have what I call the "cookie cutter" approach to interpreting. Basically, these books suggest particular events or objects in dreams have specific meanings.

Some of that can be accurate. However, from my travels throughout the world, I have found that certain symbols which are easily understood by Americans are not viewed in the same light by people from another culture.

I often listened to Bob Jones interpret visions and dreams in services over the years. Occasionally, he would come up with the craziest understanding. "Where on earth did he get that?" I asked myself on more than one occasion.

But the person Bob was speaking to was usually weeping and shaking under the power and presence of the Lord. Without question, he was uncannily accurate in hearing from heaven about that person.

From watching Bob, I learned to begin asking the Lord for interpretation and revelation about any vision or dream I was told. And God began wonderfully answering those prayers.

For instance, on a recent trip to Colombia one of our workers was a young woman who told me about a dream she was continually having. "I keep dreaming about washing my hair and using all different types of shampoo," she said. "No shampoo seemed to be right."

Several team members offered her ideas about the dream's meaning using the "cookie cutter" approach but none seemed to have it right.

Finally, I asked the Lord about its meaning, and He promptly responded. "The dream is about the men in her life and she has not found the right one yet."

When I told her what the Lord had said to me, she beamed joyfully. "That's exactly right." I knew she was on the right road for good direction in her life.

Learning from Peter's Vision

As previously mentioned with Peter's visionary ex-perience in Acts 10—and recorded a second time in Acts 11—the apostle was *greatly perplexed in mind as to what the vision"* meant, so he sought God for days until understanding was given.

Those answers for Peter began as he *"was reflecting <u>on the vision</u>, the Spirit said to him, 'Behold, three men are looking for you. But get up, go downstairs and accompany them without misgivings, <u>for I have sent them Myself'</u>,"* (Acts 10:19-20).

Visions & Dreams

At Cornelius' house, Peter connected his vision of being exhorted to eat non-kosher food with associating or being in the home of a Gentile (Acts 10:29). *"I most certainly understand now that God is not one to show* partiality," he said (Acts 10:34).

Prior to that vision, Peter was intolerant of Gentiles as most Jews were. But his obedience to that vision radically changed the history of the Body of Christ.

How does a person obtain understanding of visions and dreams?

I believe it begins with learning to obey the Word of the Lord in our individual lives. There is no substitute in obeying God's instructions.

But there are also some practical steps. I enourage people to get a journal and write down the visions and dreams that occur in their lives. We should also record those things the Lord speaks in our times of prayer and devotion. In my own life, I *daily* write down the words that God speaks to me. It is one of the greatest sources of encouragement.

Take note of the Biblical promises God calls to your attention. Keep them before your eyes and in your mouth so that you can pray over them knowing He will bring them to pass in your life.

Chapter 6

Questions & Answers

"In the first year of Belshazzar king of Babylon Daniel saw a dream and visions in his mind as he lay on his bed; then he wrote the dream down and related the following summary of it."

--Daniel 7:1 (NASB)

Often, I'm asked challenging questions about dreams and visions after a service, and I'd like to share some of those significant questions and answers in this chapter.

Q. I have a lot of really intense dreams that are bad. Not only that, but the dreams seem to affect me during the daytime. What advice could you give me in such a situation about negative dreams?

A. I would say to actively sanctify your dreams and your imagination before you go to bed. That's a prayer I suggest that you pray over yourself at bedtime. Further, I would pray for the *"discerning of spirits"* about these dreams. See 2 Corinthians 10:2-5 for some instructions on *"taking every thought captive to the obedience of Christ."*

For instance, there was a season in my own life where I wrestled with thoughts of having a serious automobile accident. I couldn't seemingly get those thoughts out of my mind

Those thoughts troubled me for many months until one day I spoke up. "I rebuke these thoughts in the Name of Jesus and I forbid that from happening to me." And I verbally claimed the blood of Jesus over myself and my car.

The thoughts went away only to return a few days later. It wasn't an instant success but gradually there was a change. In time I was absolutely freed from that torment which had seemingly dogged my path for a long time.

Q. From your personal experiences, what would be a healthy discipline to embrace in stewarding visions and dreams? I had two very vivid dreams years ago which I have written down but they remain unfulfilled. Am I missing something here?

A. Regarding dreams and visions, you don't try to make anything happen, but you position yourself by developing greater intimacy with the Father. Truthfully, the more intimate you become with God, the more He can trust you with more of the riches and more of the mysteries of heaven.

Questions & Answers

In my former devotional life, I never got still or quite enough to listen to God's voice. Of course, I read the Bible and prayed. I could quote all kinds of Bible verses but I did not know Him in a real, experiential way. Whatever God has for you in this life is all birthed out of that deeply-personal and intimate relationship with Him.

We need to understand that God seldom calls us to tasks that we can easily do within our own selves. He always seems to call us to step into uncharted territory that requires absolute dependency upon Him. Developing an intimate relationship with the living God sounds simple but it can be the hardest thing you've ever done in your life.

Q. When I have dreams and visions, sometimes I feel that I am being prepared for things to come. For instance, I had a dream that my grandson had been in a car accident. I called a friend and we immediately prayed together over the dream declaring "this will not happen." Two weeks later, my friend's grandson *actually* had an accident.

A. Well, you did exactly the right thing in praying protection into that situation because the enemy obviously wanted to take that young man out. The fact that it was her grandson and not yours is almost immaterial, because God took control of the situation with your prayers. You correctly discerned that you needed to pray over that dream.

Q. I've had a vision about someone being healed who is presently taking chemo treatments. Others are praying for her as well. Would it be unbelief for me to continue praying since I already know she will be healed?

A. Of course, you should continue praying and thanking God for manifesting this woman's healing. You are actually re-enforcing what you were shown in the vision.

Q. In the case of dreams, are they all symbolic or literal?

A. Joseph's interpretation of Pharaoh's dream (Genesis 41:25-36) is probably the best known in Scripture. If all dreams were literal, Pharaoh would have needed to go into farming, or running a dairy or operating an ice cream store.

However, the dream was symbolic, and required divine interpretation. The dream's understanding would have been impossible to discern otherwise, and fortunately Joseph was skilled in that area.

Q. I have been praying and asking God to show me why I have not been healed in a particular area of my life. Today, when we had our visualization time, I saw myself in a grammar school cafeteria, and I heard myself saying, "I am here alone with Jesus."

I realized I am not alone. I am with Jesus. I also realized I had some issues of unforgiveness towards God in my life. I also heard Him say, "I was wounded for your transgressions. I was pierced for your iniquities and by My stripes, you were healed." I know my healing is coming.

Questions & Answers

A. God has the answers for every situation we face in this life. We can literally spend thousands of dollars going all over the world seeking a word from heaven. But the truth is we can get answers for ourselves by spending time in God's presence. Others can confirm what He has already put in our hearts, but God's highest and best is still the priesthood of the believer.

Chapter 7

Prayer of Activation

"I kept looking in the night visions, And behold, with the clouds of heaven One like a Son of Man was coming, And He came up to the Ancient of Days And was presented before Him."

--Daniel 7:13 (NASB)

[As you pray this prayer of activation, expect to see visions, identify them, believe them and position yourself to receive from heaven.]

Father, I thank You for Your Word on visions and dreams, and the great significance that they play in all of my life.

God, I pray for a release of visions and dreams now to become common place and an everyday experience for me.

Visions & Dreams

God, I pray for a discerning of spirits to go along with the experiences so that I can know clearly what is from You and what is not.

Lord, I will embrace those visions from You and act upon them. In the same way, I will reject those visions that are not from You in the Name of Jesus.

Father, I pray that my spiritual eyes will be opened now to see into the realm of the Spirit...to see visions on the screen of my mind.

Father, I pray that You will cause activation of all my spiritual senses—my spiritual sight, spiritual hearing that I can truly hear Your voice and hear the sounds of heaven, and the spiritual senses of taste, smell and touch.

Father, I pray for this activation in the Spirit realm to smell the sweetness of Your presence.

Father, I pray for this activation in the Spirit that I can feel Your embrace, that I can experience these fresh encounters with You.

Father, I completely yield myself to You now. I ask that you bring fresh revelation through visions in the Name of Jesus.

Prayer of Salvation

The most important decision anyone can make in life is to receive Jesus Christ as Lord and Savior. You can make that life-changing decision right now by simply praying the following prayer out loud with me:

Lord Jesus, I ask You to forgive me of my sins and to cleanse me from those things that have kept me in bondage. I surrender to you today. I ask You to come into my heart and be my Lord and Savior.

I believe that You are the Son of God and that You were raised from the dead. Thank You, for hearing my prayer and giving me a new life as a child of God.

In Your holy Name, I pray, Amen.

[If you prayed that simple prayer with me, why don't you take a few minutes and write me about your decision for Jesus.]

About the Co-author...

 **ROBERT PAUL LAMB** has preached the Gospel in some seventeen nations of the earth. However, he is best known for writing over 45 books (with over four million in print), many of which were written on the lives of exceptional men and women of God. He is the co-author of the book, Open My Eyes, Lord.

For book, CD, or MP3 orders,
please contact:

Open Heaven Publications
an outreach of Gary Oates Ministries, Inc.
P.O. Box 457/Moravian Falls, 28654 USA
336-667-2333
info@GaryOates.com

For more information, visit our website:

www.GaryOates.com